How to Attract and Get What You Really Want

Uncover the Secret to Creating a More Fulfilling Life Using the Power of Universal Laws

Ellen J. John

Copyright

ISBN: 978-1-312-04492-0

Any information provided in this book is through the author's interpretation. The author has done strenuous work to reassure the accuracy of this subject. If you wish you attempt any of the practices provided in this book, you are doing so with your own responsibility. The author will not be held accountable for any misinterpretations or misrepresentations of the information provided here.

All information provided is done so with every effort to represent the subject, but does not guarantee that your life will change. The author shall not be held liable for any direct or indirect damages that result from reading this book.

Contents

Introduction

Wanting to change your life and changing it are two very different things. The Law of Attraction is the means to achieving your dreams because it is a new way of thinking.

We go through life focused on the wrong things and then we wish and want our lives to be different, without ever realizing that it is our own mindsets that hold us back from success. There is a theory that hard work is the only road to success; work hard and all of your goals will come true.

However, how does that account for the people who work hard, but still come up short. There is nothing more frustrating than working hard with very little to show for it but yet that is what happens to most people on a daily basis.

Hard work is only part of the equation and that is where the Law of Attraction comes in; the Law of Attraction is the second half, the correct mindset.

Let us take two examples. Steve is a sales manager; he comes to work daily with a positive attitude. It is a high energy and hectic workplace, and the sales team is constantly under pressure and that means that Steve is under a lot of pressure. If his team does not perform well, it reflects poorly on Steve. Steve comes to work daily with the mindset that his team will exceed their daily sales quota.

When a problem comes up, Steve is confident that his team will be able to handle it and he only intervenes when necessary. When any member of his team is having trouble meeting their daily quota, instead of being mad, Steve goes over different sales strategies with him. Steve is always positive towards his staff and tells them that he believes that if they have a bad day today that they will bounce back tomorrow. Steve's sales team is the top performing team for the company.

Barry is the sales manager for the same company but at another location. Barry comes into work dreading the day; expecting to barely come close to the quota. Barry never expects his team to exceed their quota; in fact, he has very little confidence in his team. Barry is known for meeting problems with yelling, and his sales team tiptoes around him. Barry works 12 hours days, hoping to try to get his team to sell more but yet they constantly fall short. Barry is filled with stress and anxiety daily and has no faith in his team, nor does he enjoy his job. Barry's team is the lowest performing sales team in the company.

Two sales managers at the same company yet one has found success and one has not, despite them both being hard workers. The difference between them is their mind set.

The way that you think determines how your life goes. If you want a different life, you need to change your thinking and the Law of Attraction is how you do that. Turn your dreams into a reality and start working smarter and you will get what you want.

The Law of Attraction is about focusing on the right things, like Steve, who focused on his team exceeding their sales quota. Barry focused on his team failing to meet the challenge, and because of that, he failed to lead them into success.

If you focus on success and combine that with hard work, you can reach your goals. If you focus on failure, not matter how much hard work you put in, you will continue to find failure because that is what you focus on.

This book will change your life as long as you are willing to change your mindset.

Law of Attraction Basics

Many people were unaware of the Law of Attraction until the movie "The Secret" came out. Thanks to it, the Law of Attraction was brought front and center to the world and interest in it spiked.

What many do not know is that the Law of Attraction is older than the "The Secret." So how old is the Law of Attraction? Well, it is as old as the universe because it is a universal law, as are all of the laws that the Law of Attraction is based on.

These laws have been in effect, working since the dawn of time; they are universal laws, static and unchanging. They were not created, they just are and that is why they work; they are not a work of fiction to be manipulated, they are laws that work in a specific fashion and once you understand how they work and why they work, you can put them to work for you.

The Law of Attraction was first written about in the 1906, when William Walter Atkinson wrote a book titled Thought Vibration or the Law of Attraction in the Thought World. Ernest Holmes was the next author to write about the Law of Attraction, titling his 1926 book Basic Ideas of Science of Mind. The next major publication about the Law of Attraction was in 1949 by Dr. Raymond Holliwell, who wrote Working with the Law.

As you can see, the Law of Attraction is not just a recently discovered phenomena but its popularity certainly did come front and center to the world in the 1990s. Jerry and Esther Hicks really brought the Law of Attraction to light during the 1990s and through them; thousands of people learned about the Law of Attraction and improved themselves and their lives.

The more people who discovered how the Law of Attraction worked and that it did work, the more they talked about it and so the Law of Attraction continued to gain in popularity. The Law of Attraction has been proven to be effective.

Simply put, if the Law of Attraction did not work, it would not be as popular as it is. There are people who say that it does not work and that it is a hoax. The people who claim the Law of Attraction did not work are the people who did not use it correctly.

There is an incorrect assumption among the uninformed that the Law of Attraction means that you can get what you want simply by thinking about it. This is incorrect.

Nothing happens unless you work for it. This is not a get rich quick scheme and the people who try to use it as such will find that it does not work. The Law of Attraction will help you get wealthy, if that is what you desire, or to get a better job, better health or even a better relationship but you still have to put in the work!

If you think that you can just wish for money and sit back, waiting for it to fall into your lap, this book will not help you. If you are willing to learn a new way of thinking and to put in the work needed to fulfill your goals and dreams, this is the book for you.

What is the Law of Attraction exactly? Although it has been worded in many different ways by many different people, what it breaks down into is that you are the creator of your own reality.

What you think about influences your reality, so by changing your thoughts, you can change your reality. What you are thinking about is what you bring into your life; another way to put it is that like attracts like.

That is the basics of the Law of Attraction and notice that it says that what you are thinking about is what you attract into your life. It does not mention that it has to be good. If you are thinking about something negative, you will be attracting more negativity into your life.

The Law of Attraction does not discriminate against what you want and what you do not want, it only focuses upon the thoughts that you are projecting into the world.

That is why the Law of Attraction is a new way of thinking. Change your thoughts and you can change your reality, for the better. You see, so often we focus on what we do not have instead of what we want and that is our downfall. Here is an example of how like attracts like.

May is a sales clerk at a local shop. May barely makes enough money to pay her bills, and she is falling behind in credit card debt. During her shift, May worries about not being able to pay her bills and that she will slide further into dept.

When May gets home, she dreads the mail, knowing that she will have more bills. May worries daily about not having enough money. May is distracted when at work, and despite working long hours and working extra shifts, she still struggles to pay her basic bills.

Jane is another sales clerk at a local shop. Jane makes the same wage as May, and paying bills on time is not always possible. Jane does have credit card debt and like May, it weighs on her mind. Jane decided to change, using the Law of Attraction, Jane starts thinking of the money that she will earn through sales. When the bills come in, Jane is grateful that she has enough money to pay them and is happy to do so. Jane is attentive at work and customers love her; soon Jane had her debts paid and she was able to start saving money.

May, focused on a lack of money and it kept her locked into a cycle of not having enough money. Jane broke out of that cycle using the Law of Attraction. She stopped focusing on what she did not have and instead focused on what she did have, which was enough money to pay for the basic bills.

Jane's attitude was better thanks to this and when combined with her hard work, money was no longer a problem. You can see how this is not a get rich quick scheme, this is a change your entire life way of thinking. Instead of being May, you can choose to be Jane.

You can manifest the things that you want into your life by your thoughts. Thinking about the wrong things, will only bring more of the things that you do not want into your life.

By changing your focus, you can achieve great things because you will be attracting the things that you want and need into your life instead of what you do not want. Negative thought cycles will keep negativity in your life and positive thought cycles will bring you positive things.

What do you want more of in your life, negative or positive? The choice is clear; everybody wants more positive things in their life. You want more positive things in your life or you would not have picked up this book.

Your mind is a powerful tool and this book will unlock your potential. The universe is made up of energy. Everything that you see and touch is made up of energy and the things around you that you cannot see or touch are also composed of energy.

When you think, your thought waves act as energy, putting energy vibrations out into the universe.

That energy attracts similar energy; bringing it into your life. This is how the Law of Attraction works and why Jane was able to start seeing more money in her account instead of less.

By focusing the money she had, she was thinking positively, and more money was attracted to her. May, on the other hand, was thinking only of the money she did not have and so because she focused on the lack of money, she continued to attract a lack of money in her life.

The Law of Attraction will bring you what you want, provided that you follow these guidelines and believe in the system. If you do not have an open mind, this will not work for you. You need to think and expect that the Law of Attraction will work for you and it will.

The 11 Forgotten Laws

The Law of Attraction is just one law out of 11 laws whose principles are used to make the system work. The Law of Attraction actually involves 11 laws, which are referred to in this book as the 11 forgotten laws. Why the forgotten laws?

In this book, they are referred to as the forgotten laws because so many people and so many places teach about the Law of Attraction without teaching about all of the 11 laws that make the Law of Attraction work. These 11 laws are often forgotten about, seen as just background material. Instead of focusing on just a single law, the Law of Attraction, all 11 laws are used together.

However, in this book, nothing is background material and it is all-important. When you skip and choose what parts of the Law of Attraction that you are working with, you are trying to take a short cut and short cuts get you nowhere quickly.

The quickest way to success is not by skipping steps but by learning and understanding a concept totally. The Law of Attraction is more than just positive thinking, visualization and a change of focus, it is a total system and for it to work for you, you need to know all of the basics, including the 11 forgotten laws.

Many sites and books skip over these because they want to get right to the meat and bones of the Law of Attraction but that does you no favors. The Law of Attraction is just one law of many. Because it is simpler to just include the other laws in teachings about the Law of Attraction that is how many handle it; but this chapter will go over all of the laws.

Without an in-depth understanding of all of the laws that make up what is known as the Law of Attraction, it will never work as well as it could. Each one of the laws is important because they are the foundation upon which the Law of Attraction works upon.

You will see in the later chapters how all of these laws combine to help you attract and get what you want out of life.

Law of Thinking

The Law of Thinking is that your state of mind will be how your reality is. Your reality is shaped by how you think and what you think about. If you go out into public in a bad mood, scowling and frowning at everybody you encounter, you will get mostly scowls and frowns back.

If you go out with a smile, you will get mostly smiles back. Whatever you are thinking or whatever the state of your mind is, that is the reality that you create around you. Think positive and the universe gives you positive things in respond but if you think negative, you will find that the universe gives you negativity back.

Knowing that what you think is important, you can now begin to change your thinking to change your life. Learning to control your thinking means that you can begin to control your life. If you do not want to invite something into your life, do not think about it. You can greatly influence the world around you simply by changing how you think.

The Law of Thinking can be applied to your home life, your work life and your relationships. Think back on the last time that some unexpected problem came up and you reacted with frustration. It made it longer and harder to sort out the problem because you were frustrated.

Now, imaging tackling that same problem with the mindset that you can and will solve the problem; it will not make the problem go away, but it will allow you to solve it easier and with less stress.

Law of Supply

The Law of Supply says that the universe has already created all that we need. None of our wishes and desires is being drawn from a finite resource pool. The universe is infinite and there is an abundance of supply for all that we want, as long as we want it.

The key here is that there are infinite resources to provide us with what we want, as long as we want it. We need to want it and we need to ask for it. If there is no demand, the universe will not be able to supply anything to us. If we demand it by asking for it, then there are plenty of resources to supply us with what we need.

In other words, going back to a prior example, Jane receives money because she asks for it by thinking about having more money. If May did the same thing, she would have also received enough money to pay her bills. The universe is not on a first come first served basis, there is enough supply for everybody who asks.

We live in a competitive society; we are raised to be the best and that other people are always nipping at our heels to take what is ours from us. However, this is not true. We are not in competition with other people to get what we want, as long as we ask for it; it is already there, waiting for us. The universe has an abundance of resources readily available.

Somebody else will not fail to get the perfect job that they desire because you got your perfect job first. If you get a raise, it does not mean that somebody else asking for raise gets denied. There is enough for everybody, they just need to ask and it is not selfish of them to ask because the supply is already there.

The Law of Supply is a shift in perception from things being scarce and lacking, to things being abundant. When you follow the Law of Supply, all things exist in abundance so instead of competing, you are just doing the best that you can, for yourself.

If you want something, ask for it and accept it without guilt. When you are given something that you ask for, it was not given to you leaving somebody else wanting, it was given to you because you asked and it came to you.

Instead of feeling frantic, as if you need to hoard what is given to you, you live happy, secure in the knowledge that whatever you use, the universe will provide back. People who live by the Law of Supply are those that share happily, they enjoy what they have instead of just wishing they had more.

Law of Attraction

This has already been discussed, the Law of Attraction is the law that says that what we think about, we attract. The principle of like attracting like is the center point of this law. The Law of Attraction is the law that most people focus on, even though the other 10 laws are all used together to attract and manifest what you wish and desire.

The Law of Attraction has grown to be a blanket term that covers all of the laws into one, instead of taking them all separately. Indeed, in order to manifest your desires, all 11 laws must be used.

The other 10 are the forgotten laws, falling in the shadow of the Law of Attraction. However, this chapter and the next detail the other 10 laws, giving you an understanding of what they are and how you can use them. All of the laws need to be used together; you cannot pick one or two to use and skip the rest.

Our imaginations are powerful tools and when combined with our thoughts, we can manifest the things that we want, bringing them into our lives. Whatever you want, it is yours; you just have to envision it being yours. This is more than just thinking about it once, you have to keep it in your mind constantly, so that you are always thinking about it and then it will happen.

This constant thought, it is how you attract your desires to you. It works in many ways but mostly, because you are always thinking of what you want, when an opportunity presents itself, you are more apt to take it because you have been looking for it.

Opportunities pass us by all the time because we are not looking for them so we let them pass by, without realizing that we just passed on the means to achieving our dreams.

Law of Receiving

The Law of Receiving has a slightly misleading name because it is about giving just as much as it is about receiving. The Law of Receiving says that in order to receive, you must first be willing to give.

Whatever you are asking the universe for more of, you need to freely give that same thing. If you want a better relationship, then you must be a better relationship partner. If you want to learn a new skill or improve yourself, be willing to help others improve and learn as well. If you want more money, be willing to give money, without resentment.

You must freely give in order to open to receiving. In such a materialistic society, we always think we need more and with that mentality, we hoard what we have, unwilling to share it with those who are in need. If you are unwilling to help out, the universe will not help you out.

You cannot be selfish and still expect to receive what you are asking for. It simply does not work like that. If you want to receive, you must first give and you need to give with an open heart and an open mind. If you are giving, but are angry about it; your resentments will prevent you from receiving.

The more you are willing to give then the more the universe will see fit to reward you with. There are countless opportunities that arise daily that you can give to others, in many small ways. Drop money in a tip jar, give the waitress an extra couple of dollars, lend some money to a good friend, help a co-worker with a problem at work, help your neighbor with his home project and always be willing to share a smile; these are just a few ways in which you can give and it will open you up to being able to receive.

Law of Increase

The Law of Increase says that when you start to praise something, it grows. You can praise your own self-esteem, somebody else's, a car that you want, a dream job or even money and because you have praised it, it will grow. Praising is not worshipping; so you cannot covet and worships money but if you praise it by thinking of it in highly favorable terms, you will be growing money and inviting it into your life.

Whatever you want more of in your life you must praise it. Let us go back to money for a minute; if you think of it in bad terms, why would the universe provide you with something that you do not like?

Praise means that you are open to receiving something and when you are thinking negatively about something, you are telling the universe that you do not want that thing, no matter what it might be.

Insincere praise will not work. It has to be praise that is open and honest, coming from your heart. If you are not the type to see the good in all people and things, this maybe a struggle for you but all it takes is a change of how you think. Start being grateful for what you have and praising it and that will allow more of what you want to come into your life. Praise is a very powerful thing and you should praise everything that comes to you.

This means that you need to banish any negative thoughts, because those will work against you and against the Law of Increase. Remember, there is an abundance of supply in the universe, and as long as you are positive, are open and are grateful, things will come your way.

The 11 Forgotten Laws – Part 2

Five of the 11 forgotten laws were discussed in the prior chapter. This chapter will discuss the remaining six laws including what they are and how they will help you manifest your wants and desires into a reality.

Remember, all of these forgotten laws should be used together in order for you to successfully manifest what you want into your life.

Law of Compensation

The Law of Compensation is also known as the Law of Cause and Effect and it says that what we are compensated with is a direct result of what we give. This is a notion that is closely related to Karma, what goes around comes around.

Compensation has nothing to do with actual payment; but rather anything that the universe provides to you is compensation. If you are kind, you receive kindness back but if you treat others badly, expect to be treated badly in return.

Every deed that you do is returned to you in kind so if you want good things to manifest for you, you need to put positive and good things out into the world. Does this mean that if you are kind and good that bad things will never happen to you?

No, but in the end, it will be evened out. Whatever you want out of life, you need to give that as well. You cannot shower people with scorn and demand respect. If you want respect, you give respect and you will get it in return.

This can be a challenge in your daily life because it is easy to take things too personally. Somebody having a bad day can take it out on you and you might react badly, because you take what they say as a personal attack, when it really is not. However, you cannot control the actions of others; only your reactions so instead of taking things personally, control your reactions and do not respond in a negative way.

At first, learning to constantly be positive and to react positive, especially in the face of adversity is hard, but once you get into the habit, you will see that your life is improving and that more good things are coming to you with your new way of thinking and reacting.

Remember, the Law of Attraction requires work. You do not sit back and reap rewards, if you want to manifest your desires, you need to put forth the work and you will be compensated. Nothing comes free and nothing comes easy.

The Law of Compensation means that the more work you put in, with the right mindset, the more will come back to you.

Law of Non-Resistance

The Law of Non-Resistance simply states that whatever you resist in your life will persist in your life. If you hate or dislike something, that thing will linger in your life. Why?

Because when you hate or dislike something to the point of thinking about it, you are manifesting it in your life by continuing to think about it. For instance, if you are in a job that you do not like, your life will be miserable. You will wake up dreading going to work, you will be miserable all day at work and by the time you get home, you will be grumpy about having been at work, at a job you did not like. Your days are nothing but a cycle of misery.

If you have a job that you do not enjoy, instead of hating it, accept that you may not like this job but that it is your job. Accept that unless a better opportunity arises that you need to accept your present job and not resist it daily and you will find that although you may not love your job, that you can certainly tolerate it and even begin to like it.

Non-resistance does not mean that you never fight for what you want; it is a way to overcome your challenges without causing yourself stress. You can apply the Law of Non-resistance to your work, to your bank account, to your relationship partner and to anything. If you are in debt, being angry about it will not help you get out of debt.

Letting go of the anger and the worry will help you cultivate a better mindset, which will help the other laws help you manifest the money that you need.

When something happens, use the Law of Resistance to temper your reaction, or rather your non-reaction. In the prior law, it was mentioned that if somebody said something to you in anger, because they had a bad day, it is tempting to react in anger but do not.

You will never win an argument with somebody who wants to argue, because they do not intend to change their mind, they just want to argue so do not even engage. Same with any situation take the path of non-resistance and it will prevent anything negative from taking root in your life.

Law of Forgiveness

When we harbor resentments, it holds us back and keeps us from growing and being positive. The Law of Forgiveness states that not only must we forgive others but we must forgive ourselves as well.

For many people, the mistakes of their past are like quicksand, sucking them into a cycle of blame and it is hard to break out of. You need to not only forgive others, to let go of resentments and bad feelings, but you need to forgive yourself for any mistakes that you have made in your past.

Your past does not define you, unless you let it. So stop letting it. Everybody makes mistakes, and if you want to have a better life, you need to forgive. Forgive opens you up to being open to possibilities and opportunities that you would not feel if you held negative feelings in your heart and soul.

Negative emotions like grief, anger, despair and resentment help us from seeing the truth. For example, if somebody in a red car cut you off, causing you to get into an accident; you have a right to be upset at the driver of that car. However, if you start to resent or be suspicious of anybody in red car after that, to the point of even being hostile, that is not a good way to live your life and you will be inviting more negativity into your life.

However, if you forgive that one driver, you will no longer view anybody who drives a red car with suspicion.

Your energy should always be directed towards something positive, where it will do good, instead of towards something negative, where it will only hold you back. Forgiveness is freedom and the way towards abundance and positive thinking.

Law of Sacrifice

In order to get what you want, you need to be disciplined and that is where the Law of Sacrifice comes in. If you want something done, you need to take some sort of action to make it happen; you need to have the discipline to do something about it and that means giving up something. For example, if you want more money, you need to work hard for it; if you want to learn how to paint, you need to take time to learn; if you want to find a better job, you need to sacrifice some time towards looking for it.

Nothing comes without paying a price. It has been stated before in this book that if you are looking for a way to get easy money or if you expect a big payoff without being willing to do the necessary work then this is the wrong book for you.

When it comes time to take action, it is so easy to make excuses instead of just doing what needs to be done. The Law of Sacrifice means that you stop making excuses and you do what needs to be done to meet your goal.

If your goal is to get out of debt, but you spend at least $100 on clothing a month, and at least $300 on eating out, if you want to get out of debt, give up your spending habits. Do you need to have a $5 latte daily? Not if you want to get out of debt.

Nothing comes without some sort of sacrifice and if you are serious about manifesting what you most want out of life, you need to make some changes and that includes some sacrifices. If you are not willing to give up anything, you will not receive anything from the universe.

Law of Obedience

The Law of Obedience is simple, you learn about the 11 laws and you obey them. The laws exist, whether or not you believe in them. If you want to manifest what you want, you need to understand the laws believe in them and obey the laws and they will work for you, bringing you what you want. Obedience simply means that you follow the rules of the 11 laws.

If you do not have the discipline to obey the laws, you will not find great success in manifesting your desires. The laws are not there for you to use when you feel like it, you need to always use them or they will not serve you very well at all.

There is a lot of work involved in the Law of Attraction, think of the laws as steps you need to take but the payoff is huge, you get that which you most desire. There is no greater reward than that. All of the laws work together, if you follow some of them, but not all, it will cause disharmony and you will not be able to manifest what you want.

Is it easy to follow all 11 laws? No, but that is why this is the Law of Obedience. You must find the discipline within yourself to follow the laws.

If you are afraid of doing the work that the laws require of you, then you will not get what you want. It is that simple. You need to change your thinking and change your perceptions so that you follow the laws and you will find that you get what you want, with the added bonus of a better life.

Law of Success

The last law, the Law of Success; this is the law that says if you think you will succeed then you will succeed. If you expect to fail, failure will happen. If you expect to succeed, even if you do not succeed on your first try, you will persist and succeed. You have the capacity within you to manifest all of your wishes, your success rest firmly in your belief in yourself.

The universe does not limit you to one wish; you can use the Law of Attraction to manifest infinite things, as long as you follow the 11 laws. Impossible is only a word, nothing more. The Law of Success does not mean that you will find success on the first try, but when you know in your heart that you can succeed, every problem that you come across can be solved.

If you do not follow this law, when problems happen, you get flustered and stressed, you might even give up, getting angry. If you follow this law, no problem is insurmountable, you just need to persist and if you do, you succeed.

You need to persist until you succeed each and every time. Giving up is not the way to get what you want; the other laws give you all of the tools to be able to handle challenges and problems easily, keeping you on track and focused.

If you follow the 11 forgotten laws, the Law of Success will be easy because you will already have the mindset that nothing will get you down. Instead of letting opportunities pass you by because you are afraid of possibly failing, start being bold. Step out of the shadows and really take control of your life because you know that you will succeed.

Your goals are all possible, as long as you believe that they are. The only roadblock keeping you from your own dreams is your attitude and your way of thinking. Follow the 11 forgotten laws and you will start seeing the changes.

Deciding What You Want

This sounds simple but in reality, it is what many people struggle with. You need to know what it is that you want before setting out to get it. Simple, right? Not so much, actually.

We are so used to focusing on what we lack, or what we do not want that it becomes very challenging to switch our gears to identify the things that we actually want and need. This chapter will help you with the first step in attracting what you want, deciding what you want.

By now, you have learned that what you focus on and what you think about determines what you get out of life. Focus on having too many bills and you will continue to have too many bills. Focus on having a job that you like and you will be stuck in a job that you hate. Focus on not being confident enough and you will never be confident. We focus on the wrong things

Try this short exercise. Let us say that you want a new house. What is the first thing that comes to your mind? Did you immediately think of all of the things that you did not want or did you think of the things that you do want in a house? Bet you had to stop and think about that.

Let us take this example, two people, each looking for their dream home. Karen goes to the realtor and tells the realtor that she is looking for the perfect home and that these are the things that she is looking for: three or four bedrooms, large kitchen with an island, a yard with shade trees, a two car garage, fireplace, two story house, two full bathrooms, a balcony, and for there to be plenty of space for planting a garden.

Karen's realtor shows Karen a few houses and within a month, Karen has found the house of her dreams. By knowing very clearly what she was looking for, Karen was able to attract and get the house of her dreams because the realtor was able to find perfect matches.

Becky is also looking for a house; she knows she wants a house that she will love and so she sees the same realtor. Becky tells the realtor that she does not want a house that has a small garage that does not have a small kitchen, or only a single bathroom.

She also says that she wants a house bigger than two bedrooms and it has to have a nice yard but she does not want a small patio. After several months of the realtor showing Becky houses that she does not like, Becky gets frustrated. She does not understand why she is unable to find the house of her dreams.

This is a perfect illustration of how the first part of the Law of Attraction works; you have to know what you want. If you know what you want, as Karen did, you will find that the Law of Attraction works better when you clearly identify your desires and goals. If you do not, much like Becky, you will have a long and frustrating journey that will most likely end in failure.

So is knowing what you do not want useless? Absolutely not. In fact, you can use what you do not want to help develop a crystal clear vision of what you do want. The concept of contrast, which when used in the Law of Attraction, means anything that makes you not feel happy, does not invoke a good mood, causes a negative reaction or is something that you just plain do not like.

Why is knowing what you do not want important? Because you can use contrast to develop a clear picture of what you do what.

The minute you find yourself thinking about something that you do not like, you need to stop yourself and then think about that thing in terms of what you do like. Look at Becky, in the above. Becky told the realtor that she did not want a small patio, for Becky, that small patio was in contrast to what she wanted, which was a large patio, big enough for a barbeque, tables, chairs and planters that she could plant in.

However, instead of saying what she wanted, making the realtor's job easier, she only said what she did not want.

The Law of Attraction gives you what your think about the most. If you think about what you do not want, it gives you what you do not want and that is why some people feel that the Law of Attraction does not work. However, the Law of Attraction works just fine, as long as you change your thinking so that you think about what you want, not in terms of what you do not want!

Pinpoint Your Desires

The difference between the people who have success with the Law of Attraction and those who do not largely hinges upon that person's ability to identify what they want out of life.

Everybody can come up with an immediate list of things that we do not want and things that make us miserable daily but when they have to give an example of what they most want in this world, they pause. It is not a positive sign of our society when people can easily come up with a list of things that they do not want instead of a list of what they do want more of.

You might know that your life is not going the way you want it; perhaps you wish you had more money, or that your health was better, a new car or house or maybe you just wish you had a better job, more confidence or a better relationship.

However, better is too vague. You want a better job than what you have now? Better how? Better is not specific and with the Law of Attraction, vague will not give you results that you find satisfactory.

Here is an example. Jerry is unhappy with his job; the hours are long and the pay is not very much. Jerry does not enjoy going to work so Jerry decides to use the Law of Attraction to get a job that he likes better. Jerry is very good with dealing with people, but he does not enjoy his telephone sales job. Jerry makes a list of the things that his perfect job would have such as face-to-face interaction with people, a salary of at least $40,000, a schedule that lets him continue to spend time with his family in the evening and weekdays, a job where he is not driving 30 miles to work each way.

Jerry knows specifically what he is looking for in his job and he focuses on finding a job that fits those parameters. Jerry sees himself working very happily in a job like that and he thinks about it often, holding the thought in his mind.

Two months later, Jerry gets a job offer from a major company who hires Jerry for their public relations department, with a salary of $50,000, the company is less than 15 miles away from Jerry's house and he will have plenty of family time.

Bill also works for a company doing telephone sales. Although Bill enjoys working with people, as a telemarketer, the response he gets is usually less than positive. Bill is paid the minimum wage plus commission, but making sales is hard. Bill has to drag himself to work every morning, dreading another 10-12 hour day at work, just trying to get some commission money.

Bill decides to use the Law of Attraction as well but instead of a clear picture of what he is looking for in a job; Bill just focuses on a better job. When you ask for something vague, you get vague results and

Bill's request to the universe was answered with a ten-cent raise of his base pay.

When asking the universe for something, you need to ask very clearly. So, we now come full circle back to the big question of what do you want. The Law of Attraction will bring your goals and dreams into reality, once you identify what they are.

The Law of Attraction is here to work for you, but you need to steer it into the right direction. Think of it like a car, you guide your car, and it does not automatically know where you want to go. The Law of Attraction is like a car, it is there to help you reach your goal, you just need to steer it in the right direction.

In the beginning of the chapter, it was stated that you could use what you do not want to help you identify what you do what. Here is an example of what Bill could have done to find a job that he loved.

Bill could have made a list of all of the things that he did not like about his job:

- Minimum wage + commission = not enough money to live on
- Days that are over 8 hours long
- High stress work environment
- Very little management support

- Cold calling customers
- No benefits

Now, to narrow down a job that is a better fit, Bill could have used contrast to list the characteristics that he wanted in a job:

- No cold calling
- 8 hour work days
- Good work environment with management support
- Salary not hourly
- Benefits

Do you see how you can turn a list of what you do not want into a list of what you do want? This is how you can identify what you really want.

Now, you need to begin to decide how you want the Law of Attraction to help you. The Law of Attraction can be used to attract material things, help you improve yourself, help with health, love and your career or for money.

You do not have to pick and choose what areas you are going to ask for help in, there is no limit as to what the universe provides to you, remember the Law of Supply says that there are infinite resources. However, for the Law of Attraction to work the best, you need to pick one thing at a time to focus on.

What are your goals that you want to achieve? Take a long, hard look at yourself and your life. The easiest way to decide what you want to attract is to start with a list of the things that make you unhappy currently.

Make a list of all of the things that you are unhappy about with yourself, your job, your relationship (if you are not in a relationship, use your last relationship as an example), your financial situation, your health, and the material things around you, such as being unhappy with your house, apartment, car, etc.

Do not worry, if the lists end up being long, the longer the better because when each list is done, you will make another list based off of your first list. Take the things that you are unhappy with and on the second list, write down what you want instead.

If you do not have enough money in your bank to pay your bills, write down on your second list how much money you need to have monthly to pay your bills. If you do not have a dog but want one, on the second list, write down what kind of dog you want. If you do not have a specific breed in mind, write down the characteristics that you want, such as a friendly dog, gets along with other pets, loves to play, can go on runs with you, will protect your yard.

For every list, go through and turn your “do not want” into a second list of things that you do want.

For every item on your do want list, make it specific. If you have to write down several things, like about the dog, then do so. Your goals need to be as specific as you can make them because the next step is manifesting your desires, and that means that you will be using visualization to help, and unless you have something specific to visualize, you will be too vague in your wishes for satisfactory results.

Manifest Your Desires

Once you have a clear list of your goals and desires, you can begin to use the Law of Attraction to manifest them. There is more to the Law of Attraction than simply thinking about something and it comes to you; that is an oversimplified and incorrect myth about the Law of Attraction that continues to endure.

By learning about the 11 forgotten laws, you are aware of how the Law of Attraction works and the mechanics behind it. Knowing how the laws work gives you a framework that you can build upon.

The prior chapter helped you build your foundation, your list of very specific things that you want to manifest. Take a look at your list and make sure that it is specific enough. If you rushed through the prior chapter, it will not work.

This is not a get rich quick plan or a get what you want for no work plan. Unless you sit down and pinpoint your exact desires, you will not get what you want. There are no shortcuts to the Law of Attraction. If you are ready to take the next step, keep reading.

In order to manifest your desires, you need to do more than just think about what you want; you need to focus your energy towards it, giving it plenty of attention. Your thought waves are energy, this is the energy that goes out in to the universe and this energy is what attracts things to you.

This is why when you have negative thoughts that negative things come your way and people react to you negatively; they are responding to your negative vibrations. When you are giving off positive vibrations, then you get a positive response from the universe.

You have two kinds of thinking, conscious and unconscious. Your conscious thinking is when you are actively thinking; it is that part of your brain that you are using when you read, watch TV, have a conversation or are doing anything that requires you to think about it.

Your subconscious is where your vibrations come from because it is what sets your predominate thinking. In order to manifest your desires, you need to attune your thinking so that you are sending out vibrations about what you want, which means that you need to get your subconscious thinking in line with your desires.

You cannot improve your career, financial situation or attract anything if you write down your list of desires and then stash it in your sock drawer, or save it as a file in your computer and never give it another thought.

The Law of Attraction works as long as you do the work that is needed to get it to manifest your desires and that is the focus of this chapter; how to turn your wishes into reality by changing your thinking in order to change your vibrations, so that you are sending out vibrations that bring you what you want, instead of what you do not want.

The first thing about manifesting your desires is that you need to erase negative thinking patterns. Everybody is guilty of negative thinking every now and then, but if your thinking is usually negative and not positive, you will not be able to manifest anything.

You need to start being aware of how you are thinking. Are you the type of person who assumes that a probably outcome will be negative instead of positive? Do you have more complaints than positives to say? Are you generally happy or generally unhappy?

Happy people are not people who have no troubles, they are people who manage to be happy, despite their troubles and that is the type of person that you need to be in order for the Law of Attraction to work.

Start monitoring your thinking and erase negative thoughts before you voice them. If something makes you unhappy, does complaining solve anything? No, stop complaining and take action instead. If it is something beyond your control, let it go. A good way to help achieve this is through positive affirmations. Affirmations help you turn your thoughts around so that you are replacing negative thoughts and doubts with healthy and positive thoughts.

For example, if you want a better job but you have low self-esteem, you might think that you are not good enough to get a job with better pay or better conditions; perhaps you think that you are unable to learn the skills needed to move higher up on the career ladder. These thoughts are negative and self-destructive.

Using Affirmations

Take a look at your list of desires, goals and wishes. What negative thoughts or self-doubts come to mind when you look at each of your desires.

Write down the negative thoughts that come to mind because you are going to use contrast once again to write a list of affirmations that will absolutely erase those negative thoughts from your conscious and your subconscious thinking.

When you replace the negative thoughts with the positive ones, thanks to the affirmations, you will be sending out the right vibrations to manifest your desires. Your subconscious will be thinking only in terms of success, and you will be giving off the right vibrations that will manifest your desires for you.

How do you write affirmations? Look at your self-doubts; they are all in the present tense so you need to re-write them as positive affirmations, while keeping them in the present tense. This is where many people go wrong because they are working towards a goal that they have not achieved yet; they want to put the affirmations in a future tense.

Let us use Steve as an example. Steve would like to move up from account support to being an account manager but the account manager position requires him to travel, holding meetings and giving presentations. Steve is not a good public speaker and he is using the Law of Attraction to be a better public speaker and to be more confident so that he can get the account manager job. Steve writes the following affirmations:

- I will learn to not be nervous
- I will be better at speaking in public
- I will be able to hold meetings with others

Steve says his affirmations several times a day but he is not getting any benefit. Finally, Steve asks a friend who is familiar with the Law of Attraction and finds out that his affirmations are written wrong.

They need to be in the present tense, as if they have already been achieved and they need to be specific instead of general and vague. Steve re-writes his affirmations as:

- I am not nervous when I need to speak to people that I do not know
- I am not nervous when I hold meetings
- I am good at holding meetings
- I am good at giving presentations

Steve finds that with these new affirmations, he begins to be less nervous about speaking in public and that he is more comfortable speaking up in company meetings. His boss takes notice of how

Steve is participating in the meetings and recommends that he apply for the account manager position.

Write your own affirmations so that they are very specific to your desires and so that they are in the present tense. Yes, those are things that you want but write your affirmations as if they are true.

Every day, several times a day, you need to tell yourself your affirmations and soon, you will see that they are coming true. The power of thinking will be working for you.

In addition to your affirmations, you need to visualize your desires. To visualize, you need to imagine, very clearly, what your desires are. Just like your affirmations, you need to visualize it as being real and that it has already happened.

For example, if you want a better relationship, envision yourself on a date, with the type of partner that you want to be with. The trick to visualizing is that you need to make it like an interactive movie instead of a static picture so add elements from all of the senses to your visualization.

See yourself at dinner, on a patio in the summer so you can feel the breeze across your face and arms. See yourself eating, and envision how the food tastes, or how the wine tastes in your mouth. See yourself laughing, smiling and more importantly, your partner doing the same.

All of the specific characteristics that you want in a partner put those into your visualized partner. The more details you add, the more success you will have.

Focus on one desire at a time and throughout the day, envision that desire or wish as already being granted. See how happy it makes you and see it as if it has happened already; make it real and think of it as being real. The more real you make your visualizations, the easier it will be for the universe to manifest your wishes.

Another tool that many find useful is a vision board. A vision board is a way to have a physical representation of your desires, so every time you see your board, you think of what you want to attract.

The more you hold it in your mind, the easier it will be to attract. Print out pictures that represent all of the things that you want and set it where you can see it. Put versions of your vision board in various places of your house, on the dashboard of your car, and even at work. Create a virtual vision board with your phone, and pull up the photos that represent what you want so you can keep it fresh in your mind.

Exercises for Manifestation

Here are a variety of exercises that will help you manifest your desires better. These will help ensure that you are able to not only prepare your mind for using the Law of Attraction, but to help you achieve better success with it.

Clear Your Mind

A cluttered mind is a mind that cannot focus and without focus, you cannot visualize. Stress and anxiety will keep you from being able to visualize what it is that you are trying to get and they will make it harder for you to think positive, which is necessary for your success. Life is hectic and all of that stress accumulates in our minds, where we hold onto our worries and our anxieties, even though they serve no purpose.

Daily meditation will help you clear your mind. All you need is between five and ten minutes daily for meditation; nobody is so busy that they cannot take five minutes a day to improve their mental health.

Find a quiet spot in your house. Some people like to have nature sounds in the background, or instrumental music but nothing with vocals because you want your focus to be inward, not on anything external. Sit or lay down so you are comfortable and start focusing on your breathing, taking deep breathes in from your abdomen first.

Focus only on your breathing and then starting with your head, just do a body scan and relax each part as you mentally go down your body. By the time you are done, you will be feeling relaxed.

Goal Statements

Goal statements or goal journals are great visualization tools that will work along with affirmations and vision boards. Goal statements are statements that you write out based on your desires, written in positive language and that have all of your details in them. Basically, it is your visualization in writing but they are a powerful tool for visualization.

Your first sentence is your desire, or the intention that you have. So, going back to Steve, his first sentence of a goal statement would be "I am attracting the ability to be a more confident speaker."

Now, the next section, which is the longest section, is the area where you put your details. What do you love about your desire? What will it do for you? What exactly do you want to achieve from it and why? Keep them in the present tense and positive and you can include all of the details that make this such a desire to you.

For Steve, it would something along the line of "I've decided to be a better public speaker. I love it when I give a presentation and everybody responds positively. I have good idea and it makes me feel good when I speak up at the meeting and my boss loves to hear the ideas. I love knowing that my input is valuable. I love the feeling of confidence that I get when I am speaking in a meeting and everybody is paying attention to me."

Write your own goal statements, using your detailed desire list. Notice how it is all in the present tense and that it includes all of the positive elements. If you are working towards manifesting more money, in your goal statement you need to say what you will enjoy doing with the money; if you want a house, say what you will enjoy doing with the house, such as you will love cooking for the family in your large kitchen, or holding barbeques in the yard.

Your goal statements need to be read daily, they will help keep your desires first and foremost in your mind, attuning your vibrations towards your goals, helping them to manifest.

Allow Your Desires to Manifest

Now that you know what you want and work on manifesting it, you still need to allow it into your life. Many people do not realize that they never get what they are trying to attract because they find that they are not able to allow it into their lives. Wanting something is one thing, but allowing for it to happen is something else.

This book has stated over and over again that there are no shortcuts and the Law of Attraction requires a fair amount of work on your part. Allowing requires work and the right mindset. This can be an area of struggle because the concept of allowing for things can be so hard.

First of all, a negative attitude is the first block as are self-doubts. Your affirmations will help you get over these problems, and that will help you allow your desires to become reality but that is not all.

You need to believe in the Law of Attraction. This is a system that works on belief. If you do not believe, it will not work. You can argue that since the 11 laws are fact, that even if you do not believe that they will work, that they should work for you.

That is false. If you have even the slightest doubt that any of this will work, it will taint everything that you do and even though you are putting out vibrations about getting your desires, you are also putting out vibrations at the same time that it will not work. You attract what you think and if you think that it will not work, it will never work and you have nobody to blame but yourself.

You need to have a profound belief that the Law of Attraction will work. If you think it will not, it will not work for you. If you have doubts, get rid of them. The Law of Attraction will work for you, if you allow it to and that means that you have to believe in it.

Before you have doubts, give it a chance to work. The Law of Attraction is such a big topic because it has been proven to be a good way to attract what you want in your life. If it did not work, so many people would not have such an interest in it.

Doubts destroy goals and dreams so get rid of your doubts and go into this with a clear mind, with the expectation of getting results and you will get results.

Your affirmations that you created are used to erase doubts and that is why they are important. When you doubt, you are putting a limit on your belief that something will work, or that you can achieve success. Why shoot yourself in the foot by doing all of this work and then allowing that little voice in the back of your head to say, "This will not work."

In addition to affirmations, whenever you have a negative thought or self-doubt, you need to turn it into a statement that will allow your desire to manifest instead of preventing it. If you think that you are too old to go back to school, turn that thought into a thought that there are plenty of people older than you who have gone back to school and they are successful or that there is no age limit on bettering yourself.

Every doubt can be re-framed so that it allows your desires to manifest; just get into the habit of doing so.

What are your doubts? Write down what your main doubts are and then underneath that, write them so they are positive statements that allow for your desires. Turn every doubt into a positive statement instead, something that fills you with hope and determination instead of feeling doubtful.

Make Room for Manifestation

Part of allowing is creating space to allow for your desires to manifest. If you want new things to come into your life, you need to clear out some old things first. Sometimes, all that is needed to get you into the mindset that you are ready to receive new things into your life is by shedding some clutter.

What do you have that is holding you back? Do you have anything sitting in your closet, garage or house that might be giving you negative thoughts or bad memories? If so, get rid of it! Do some housecleaning and start getting rid of anything that is extra in your life.

We attach negative emotions to things and possessions so by getting rid of these possessions, you can get rid of a lot of emotional baggage. When you do that, you are helping yourself feel and think more positive, which helps you allow your desires to manifest better.

Even if you do not have anything with negative associations in your possession, you very likely own many things that you do not use or do not need. Gather up these items and give them to charity. You will feel better, and you will have given yourself room for the new things in your life.

Another big factor is that you have to be grateful. Gratitude is very important and if you do not have a grateful attitude for what you already have, the universe will not provide you with anything else. You need to be grateful for what you have in order to allow anything new to manifest in your life.

Gratefulness is something that many people take for granted. It is easy to go through life without realizing just how many people we should be grateful for. Somebody built the car that you drive, the TV that you use, printed the book you read, provided the electricity that powers your house, built the streets and grew the food that you eat. Without other people, we would have very little indeed.

It is easy to focus on what we do not have but that is negative thinking, start being grateful for what you do have instead of complaining about what you do not have. It is easy to complain about things such as bad health, a bad relationship, or even a car that has broken down.

However, it is just as easy to be grateful for what you do have as well. Take your focus on what is going wrong or on what you do not have and fix it on being grateful for all that you do have.

Gratitude is powerful indeed. Start seeing the silver lining and you will find that you are no longer as stressed or as anxious about the things that you lack or problems that come up.

You will be happier and healthier because your stress levels will go down. This will also allow the universe to provide you with your desires, because you are showing gratitude towards what you have.

Write down all of your current problems and study it for a minute. What are the silver linings that you can see in those problems? Write them underneath each problem.

For example, if you have a car that is old and unreliable, at least you have a car. If you have a job that you do not like, at least you have a job. If you are frustrated at qualities in yourself that you want to improve, be grateful that you have identified your areas that need improved because that is the first step towards changing.

Make a list of all the things you have to be grateful for and you will be surprised at how large that list ends up being.

To help keep gratefulness in your life, start a journal. At the end of every day, write down all of the things that you are grateful for that day. No matter how bad your day was, there were some good things.

It is just a matter of changing your perspective into being grateful instead of resentful. Do this daily and you will soon see a vast change in your attitude and your happiness and more importantly, you will be allowing your desires to manifest.

Conclusion

The Law of Attraction can and will change your life. You can use it to change your career, your relationships, your health, your emotions, your financial situation, yourself and to attract material possessions into your life.

There are 11 laws, the forgotten laws, that make up the Law of Attraction, the actual Law of Attraction is only one out of eleven laws that work together to help you attract whatever you want into your life.

We are powerful beings and our thoughts are powerful. We create our own realities through the power of our thinking. By changing your thinking, you can and will change your life and that is the basis of this book. You will be able to attract what you most want in life by using this book, providing that you follow the entire book.

All of the laws work together to help you create your own reality and what kind of reality that you create is up to you; you can create a positive reality or a negative one, depending on your thinking. Positive thinking is at the core of attracting what you want.

The Law of Attraction is not magic and it is not a shortcut towards getting something for nothing. There is a lot of work involved in making the Law of Attraction to work but for those willing to do the work, who expect it to work and who allow it to work their wishes will be manifested. The Law of Attraction works for anybody and it will work for you.

There are three basic steps for the Law of Attraction. First, you need to identify what your desires are. Your desires need to be specific and detailed instead of vague. Knowing exactly what you want is the first step.

Next, you need to begin to manifest your desires into your life by using affirmations and visualization. Once again, you need to have a positive attitude and no doubts about the Law of Attraction or about yourself.

The last step is that you need to allow for your desires to manifest and you do that by believing that your desires will manifest, by being grateful and by giving room for your desires to manifest in your life. Follow these steps and you will find happiness and success.